HAL•LEONARD
INSTRUMENTAL PLAY-ALONG

AUDIO
ACCESS
INCLUDED

Speed • Pitch • Balance • Loop

TROMBONE

PIRATES OF THE CARIBBEAN

T0081506

To access audio visit:
www.halleonard.com/mylibrary

4638-7614-7850-8578

ISBN 978-1-4234-2201-3

Disney characters and artwork © Disney Enterprises, Inc.

WALT DISNEY MUSIC COMPANY

DISTRIBUTED BY

7777 W. BLUEMOUND RD. P.O. BOX 13819 MILWAUKEE, WI 53213

Visit Hal Leonard Online at
www.halleonard.com

Title	Page

THE BLACK PEARL

TROMBONE

Music by KLAUS BADELT

BLOOD RITUAL/
MOONLIGHT SERENADE

TROMBONE

Music by KLAUS BADELT

DAVY JONES PLAYS HIS ORGAN

TROMBONE

Music by HANS ZIMMER

DAVY JONES

TROMBONE

Music by HANS ZIMMER

DINNER IS SERVED

TROMBONE

Music by HANS ZIMMER

I'VE GOT MY EYE ON YOU

TROMBONE

Music by HANS ZIMMER

HE'S A PIRATE

TROMBONE

Music by KLAUS BADELT

JACK SPARROW

TROMBONE

Music by HANS ZIMMER

THE KRAKEN

TROMBONE

Music by HANS ZIMMER

Slow and steady

THE MEDALLION CALLS

TROMBONE

Music by KLAUS BADELT

ONE LAST SHOT

TROMBONE

Music by KLAUS BADELT

TO THE PIRATE'S CAVE!

TROMBONE

Music by KLAUS BADELT

TWO HORNPIPES
(Fisher's Hornpipe)

TROMBONE

By SKIP HENDERSON

Lively

Fiddle

Play

1.

2.

WHEEL OF FORTUNE

TROMBONE

Music by HANS ZIMMER

UNDERWATER MARCH

TROMBONE

Music by KLAUS BADELT